Warwickshire
Edited by Lynsey Hawkins

First published in Great Britain in 2006 by:
Young Writers
Remus House
Coltsfoot Drive
Peterborough
PE2 9JX
Telephone: 01733 890066
Website: www.youngwriters.co.uk

All Rights Reserved

© Copyright Contributors 2006

SB ISBN 1 84602 499 4

Foreword

Imagine a teenager's brain; a fertile yet fragile expanse teeming with ideas, aspirations, questions and emotions. Imagine a classroom full of racing minds, scratching pens writing an endless stream of ideas and thoughts . . .

. . . Imagine your words in print reaching a wider audience. Imagine that maybe, just maybe, your words can make a difference. Strike a chord. Touch a life. Change the world. Imagine no more . . .

'I Have a Dream' is a series of poetry collections written by 11 to 18-year-olds from schools and colleges across the UK and overseas. Pupils were invited to send us their poems using the theme 'I Have a Dream'. Selected entries range from dreams they've experienced to childhood fantasies of stardom and wealth, through inspirational poems of their dreams for a better future and of people who have influenced and inspired their lives.

The series is a snapshot of who and what inspires, influences and enthuses young adults of today. It shows an insight into their hopes, dreams and aspirations of the future and displays how their dreams are an escape from the pressures of today's modern life. Young Writers are proud to present this anthology, which is truly inspired and sure to be an inspiration to all who read it.

Contents

Alcester High School
Lauren Hughes (12)	1
Natalie Walton	2
Chris Havard (11)	3
Paige Quiney (12)	4
Sean Blyth (11)	5
Jamie Done (12)	6
Callum Kirby (11)	7
Lucy Reynolds (12)	8
Peter Bridgeford (11)	9
Naomi Van De Ven Neade (11)	10
Hayley Millard (12)	11
Joe Leahy (11)	12
Chris Hodge (12)	13
Megan Clarke (12)	14
Adam Woollacott (12)	15
Daisy Sumner (11)	16
Eleanor Burkey (12)	17
Joe Rawlings (11)	18
Katie Hoskins (12)	19
Daniel Wallace (12)	20
Poppy Roads (11)	21
Ryan Skidmore (12)	22
Aimée Stanley (11)	23
Matthew Newby (11)	24
Gemma Wadelin (11)	25
Rosalie Clark (11)	26
Becky Lee (12)	27
Chris Hill (11)	28
Amelia Hopkins	29
Philippa Buxton (12)	30
Yasmin Murphy (11)	31
Sam Precious (11)	32
Alex Frost-Head (12)	33
Jordan Clarke (12)	34
Lauren Townsend (11)	35
Liam Beck (11)	36
Charlie Stanley (12)	37

Alderman Smith School

Bethaney Smith (13)	38
Laura Watkins (12)	39
Demi Ashby (13)	40
Sophie Downes (13)	41
James Sidwell (13)	42
Eliesha Galland (13)	43
Laura Timms (13)	44
Ryan Norman (13)	45
Laura Goodenough (13)	46
Shelly-Ann Gee (13)	47
Craig Wilson (12)	48
Anna Breeze (14)	49
Judy Coloman (11)	50
Charlotte Smith (13)	51
Daniel Wilson (14)	52
James Reed (13)	53
Danielle Palmer (14)	54
Kim Osmond (14)	55
Bianca Hutchinson (14)	56
James Gallacher (14)	57
Alex Rose (11)	58
Joe Gillespie (11)	59
Nicole Teagles (12)	60
Sophie Bates	61
Alice Blackwell (12)	62
Rory Smith (13)	63
Rachael Lackenby (13)	64
Kieren Ball	65
Ruth Nelmes (14)	66
Jonathan Bell	67
Luke Edmond	68
Danielle Roper (12)	69
Rosie Jones (12)	70
Thomas Compton (12)	71
Sophie McGee (11)	72
Daniel Southworth (12)	73
Emma Higgins (12)	74
Jake Ryland (12)	75
Ellie Alexander (14)	76
Sorrin Parsons (14)	77

Holly Carpenter (14)	78
Nenagh Brady (11)	79
Kyle Ryland (14)	80
Christine Briggs (11)	81
Guy Griffiths (11)	82
Nicole Baskett	83
Bayli Jones	84
Natasha Wickett (11)	85
Bethany Marshall (12)	86

Ashlawn School

Zara Mohammed (15)	87
Nicole Hutchinson (14)	88
Muneeb-Ur-Rahman Saharan (14)	89
Karanjit Virk (15)	90
Andrew Oldroyd (14)	91
Liam Bailey (15)	92
Jessica Holton (15)	93
Victoria Taylor (15)	94
Sally Whitmore (15)	95
James Green (14)	96
James Priest (15)	97
Antony Lowe (15)	98
Jake Rugman (14)	99
Tom Pinks (14)	100
Rebecca Dandy (12)	101
Tiffany-Jade Jones & Leia-Summer Jones (11)	102
Meg Cahill (11)	103
David Hooker (15)	104
Priyan Mistry (14)	105
Zöe Baines (15)	106
Jenni Wareing (14)	107
Michael Judd (15)	108
Harry Elwell (14)	109
Catherine Clements (14)	110
Josh Cox (15)	111
Patrick Mathy (15)	112
Katy Griffiths (15)	113
Charley Picken (15)	114
Deepika Govind (14)	115
Sophie McNaughton (15)	116

Hannah Beynon (15)	117
Emma Grant (15)	118
Kayleigh Phillips (15)	119
David Railton (14)	120

Hartshill School

Samantha Richardson (12)	121
Luke Watson (11)	122
Paul Callender (11)	123
Adam King (11)	124
Charlotte Morewood (13)	125
Thomas Kidgell (12)	126
Beth Thompson (12)	127
Danielle Le Blanoq (15)	128
Stevie Hughes (15)	129
Alicia Pattinson (14)	130
Amy Jones (15)	131
Kyle Hollyman (13)	132
Paul Rowland (13)	133
Tom Smitham (13)	134
Jason Brown (13)	135
Chloe Markham (14)	136
Rachel Windross (13)	137
Ben Storer (14)	138
Sarah Proctor (14)	139
Kelly Perrett (14)	140
Shannen Mantack (14)	141
Chelsea Richter (13)	142
Danielle Purkis (14)	143
David Allison (12)	144
Ryan Lee (12)	145
Robyn Robinson (12)	146
Francesca Harris (11)	147
Abby Oakley (16)	148
Rebecca Netherton (12)	149
Rebecca Evans (12)	150
Chelsea Lackenby (12)	151
Emma Hall (14)	152
Luke Jones (14)	153
Stephanie Bates (13)	154
Callum Fawcett (13)	155

Laura Adey (13)	156
Chloe Le-Blancq (12)	157
Daniel Dainter (15)	158
Hannah Cooper (14)	159
Ross Adams (14)	160
Jessica Bird (14)	161
Laura Miller (13)	162
Keira Shetliffe (13)	163
Hayden Wright (13)	164
James McGuinness (13)	165
Ryan Bennett (14)	166
Calum Smith (14)	167

King Edward VI School
Ben Reardon (14)	168

Oak Wood School
Jonathan Newitt (13)	169
Tom Place (13)	170
Vicky Humphrys (13)	171
Stacey Harrison (14)	172
Lina Osman (14)	173

Round Oak School & Support Service
Kieran Mancini (13)	174
Andrew Murray (14)	175
Terry Lee (14)	176
Chris Cooper (14)	177
Jaspreet Reyat (12)	178
Thomas Pugh (13)	179
Kirt Lane (14)	180
Aaron Wilkinson (13)	181

Sparrowdale School
Tom Betteridge (16)	182
Shivam Sanghani (16)	183
Joel Titmus (15)	184
Callum Vickers (15)	185
Lewis Smith (14)	186
Nicole Griffiths (14)	187

Emma Edwards (14) 188
Dominic James (14) 189
Laura Gardner (12) 190
Michael Blower (14) 191
Jessica Paul (15) 192
Luke Stephens (12) 193
Kathleen Power (12) 194
James Parker (13) 195
Scott Griffiths (14) 196

Trinity Catholic School
Rebecca Swaby (15) 197

The Poems

I Have A Dream

I have a dream the world could be free,
Then we wouldn't have to use money.
I have a dream we could all like each other,
Then we would be like one another.
I have a dream the world could change,
Then it wouldn't have to rearrange.
I have a dream we could be treated the same,
Then we wouldn't have to take the blame.
I have a dream there would be no such word as hurry,
Then we wouldn't have to worry.
I have a dream.

Lauren Hughes (12)
Alcester High School

I Have A Dream

I have a dream to make the world a better place,
To make us equal in the skin and in the face.
I have a dream to win the glory and earn the pride,
Not to be lazy but get out and ride.
I have a dream to help others in need
When they are in trouble for desperate feed.
I have a dream to find the gold at the end of the rainbow,
I'll run to find it while the sun shines low.
I have a dream to be a doctor or a vet,
To look after sick patients or a poorly pet.
I have a dream to get the greatest job,
And I'll make sure I work really hard because I don't want to be a slob!
I have a dream to own a business and get really rich,
To make some cash and not be down in the ditch.
I have a dream to swim with dolphins and run with bulls,
And to hold a monkey or koala bear like some loving fool.
I have a dream to climb the highest mountain there is,
And be the fastest one up there, because I'll race in a whizz.
I have and dream to tell great stories, to be a famous writer,
I'll write and write and won't give up, to show that I'm a fighter.
I have a dream to sail the five oceans before I die,
But when I told my father all he did was sigh.
These are all my dreams, not just when I am asleep,
My dreams will become actions, my promises I will keep.

Natalie Walton
Alcester High School

I Have A Dream

I have a dream
I could live by a stream
I could hold a monkey
I could play international rugby.

I have a dream
My friends could have high self-esteem
They could not fall out
They could not give each other a clout.

I have a dream
The world could work as a team
That food is plentiful
And humans are gentle.

Chris Havard (11)
Alcester High School

I Have A Dream

I want to feel the wind in my hair
I want to see London square.
To meet the people in the race
Who are dressed up silly with a funny face.
To feel the adrenaline in my heart
And be glad that I am taking part.
When we're ready, waiting and anticipating
The race begins; it's a long way ahead
The road is so long,
But I know I can be strong.
My head is saying, *yes, keep going on*
For this is for charity, and a very special day
So come on and cheer *hip hip hooray!*

Paige Quiney (12)
Alcester High School

I Have A Dream

I have a dream,
A real dream,
Peace to the people,
Everyone full of love
And flying white doves.

I have a dream,
A real dream,
No war,
People obey the law.

I have a dream,
A real dream,
Enough food,
Everyone in a good mood.
Nobody to tease
About what they believe,
I have a dream,
A real dream.

Sean Blyth (11)
Alcester High School

I Have A Dream

I have a dream,
I dream that everyone in the world is treated the same.

I have a dream,
I dream that we could all fly in the sky.

I have a dream,
I dream that everyone in the world could live in peace and harmony.

I have a dream,
I dream that all people on the Earth could be kind, not evil.

I have a dream,
I dream that people could live forever.

I have a dream,
I dream that everyone's life is perfect.

I have a dream,
I have a dream,
I have a dream.

Jamie Done (12)
Alcester High School

I Have A Dream

I have a dream
A big dream it may seem
But it's to make poverty
Something you learn about in history
Like the plague
To never strike again.

I have a dream
For the world to be a team
To stop all wars for no real cause
To ban all weapons from being sold
Come on people
Do it for the world.

Callum Kirby (11)
Alcester High School

I Have A Dream

I have a dream
Of my family being rich.
I have a dream
That one day my mum and dad live together.
I have a dream
Of my friends and family living forever and staying young.
I have a dream
For my sisters to do well in later life and stay happy.
I have a dream
To grow up with a happy life with a nice house.
I have a dream
That one day someone in my family wins a lot of money.
I have a dream
For my dog to get better and feel happy inside.
I have a dream
That whatever I do wrong could just be forgotten as quick as lightning.
I have a dream
That one day we have very deep snow.
I have a dream
That whatever I want in life I could have although really that wouldn't
be possible.
I have a dream
To dream the good things in life.

Lucy Reynolds (12)
Alcester High School

I Have A Dream

I have a dream that people will stop destroying the rainforests
So that animals will have a safer environment.
I have a dream that poachers will not threaten animals so that
                                                                             they will live.
I have a dream that when I'm older I will be in a band
With all my mates and we will be rich and famous.
I have a dream that bullying will stop all around the world
And people will stop fighting.
I have a dream that pollution will stop
And the world will be a safer place.
I have a dream that I will have a great long life.
I have a dream that people will stop breaking into things
                                                                     and robbing stuff.

Peter Bridgeford (11)
Alcester High School

I Have A Dream

I have a dream that everyone stopped pollution and that
                                            everyone recycled.
I have a dream that everyone could give money to charity,
                                            stopping poverty.
I have a dream that our world has no litter and that there is no crime.
I have a dream that everyone loves everyone and that everyone
                                            feels safe.
I have a dream that all these puzzle pieces are put together
                                            to make the jigsaw.

Naomi Van De Ven Neade (11)
Alcester High School

I Have A Dream

I have a dream to be that bird
Gliding over the green canopies not to be heard.

Feeling the wind beneath my wings
As I hear the chorus of other birds that sing.

Flying high in the clean sweet air
Leaving the dirt and smog down there.

Swooping below the red-hot sun
Another fine day has just begun.

Then settling down at night
With the glistening silver moon in sight.

Free to do what I want to do
I have a dream, will it come true?

Hayley Millard (12)
Alcester High School

I Have A Dream

I have a dream
That the world changes
I have a dream
That nothing is the same

I have a dream
That poverty comes to a halt
I have a dream
That the world changes

I have a dream
That the world leaders
Stop and think
About the Third World poverty

I have a dream
That the world changes
I had a dream
That nothing is the same.

Joe Leahy (11)
Alcester High School

I Have A Dream

I have a dream
Where no one's mean.
The clouds go floating by
Up in the bright blue sky.

The birds go flitter flutter
The leaves rustle in the gutter.
No one has a fight
Day or night.

Racism is no longer
Yet people still do wonder.
Will it stay the same
Or will it go back to being lame?

Chris Hodge (12)
Alcester High School

I Have A Dream

I have a dream of a world where fantasies come true
A life where everyone flew.
I have a dream where poverty is no more
A planet where there is no racism for sure.
I want no bad, only good in life
Where everybody loves their children and wife.
A world where saving species isn't a mission
And where looking the best isn't a competition.
I want a world with a cure for cancer
And life is so much fun it twirls like a ballerina dancer.
I have a dream where there's a dove
It's are full of beauty, wonder and love.
Now look at those things I have said in that font
That's what I need and what I want.

Megan Clarke (12)
Alcester High School

I Have A Dream

I have a dream where people rock and roll,
The street gets full with thoughtful souls.
Bands play using all their effort,
Each having their own little method.
I stand on stage biting my nails,
The crowd's making lots of wails.
We start our song happy and cheerful
Not by any chance fearful.
My hands are strumming and the beat's loud
All I can hear is the screaming of the crowd.
My band is in the spotlight beam
Rock and roll is my dream.

Adam Woollacott (12)
Alcester High School

I Have A Dream

I have a dream for peace in the world,
Some have a dream to race and win gold.
I have a dream for no racism on the planet,
Some have dreams to play the clarinet.
I have a dream to be loved and remembered,
Some have dreams to be a fabulous shepherd.
I have a dream for world poverty to be ended,
Some have dreams not to be offended.
I have a dream to be happy and inspiring,
Some have dreams for there to be no bombing.
I have a dream to be befriended,
Some have that dream too.

Daisy Sumner (11)
Alcester High School

I Have A Dream

I have a dream to . . .

H orse ride in the Olympics,
A ltogether stop poverty,
V ery good grades in my schoolwork,
E veryone stopping global warming.

A dream is worth having,
D reams are what you think of and go for.
R emaining with you until you succeed.
E veryone has dreams,
A ltogether,
M aking things happen.

We all have dreams if I have a dream.

Eleanor Burkey (12)
Alcester High School

I Have A Dream

I have a dream that Earth is free of war
That our children suffer not the pain of violence but live a peaceful life.
This is the new generation of children
And we as a planet are not giving them
A life that we once lived, a life free of war, violence and drugs, why?
Why can't we let them live a good life?
Because this generation is revolving around a world of war
                                                      and violence
Just why are we letting that happen?

Joe Rawlings (11)
Alcester High School

I Have A Dream

I have a dream
That someone will listen
When I talk
That's my dream.

I have a dream
To save lives
Give healthy lives
That's my dream.

I have a dream
To tell my life stories
Through beautiful people
That's my dream.

I have a dream
To marry a knight in shining armour
And have joyful children
That's my dream.

Katie Hoskins (12)
Alcester High School

I Have A Dream

I have a dream
That happens when I'm a late teen
I buy an Aston Martin car
And drive near and far.

I have a dream
One that needs to be kept clean
My dream car on my drive
Oh how good it is to be alive.

I have a dream
Where I like to be seen
Driving down the highway
Such bliss, what more can I say?

I have a dream
Which gives me self-steem
Without my car my life would be dim
But as it is, I carry this great big grin.

Daniel Wallace (12)
Alcester High School

I Have A Dream

I have a dream
I can soar through the sky
But the problem is
I'm in a cage two metres high!

I have a dream
I can feel the warm breeze
But the problem is
I usually freeze!

I have a dream
I can smell the salty sea
But the problem is
I'm not even free!

So if you see me
Just let me out
Well, you'll obviously see me
Because I'll squawk and shout.

Poppy Roads (11)
Alcester High School

I Have A Dream

I have a dream of motorbiking
To become a pro
And have lots of dough.

I have a dream of motorbiking
To be on TV
And live the life of a celebrity.

I have a dream of motorbiking
To ride for fun
And live in the sun.

I have a dream of motorbiking
I'll love the thrill
I know I will.

Ryan Skidmore (12)
Alcester High School

I Have A Dream

I have a dream of my family and friends being happy

H appy are we, my friends, my family and me
A lways there for one and other
V ery special friends I have
E very day my dream is here

A nother day

D aydreamer they say
R eally I say, it's just my dream
E asy to make happen
A nother dream has come true
M orning, I am awake!

Aimée Stanley (11)
Alcester High School

I Had A Dream

I had a dream, a dream of peace.
A dream where we all lived together in harmony,
A dream with one country, one religion and one purpose.
A purpose to enjoy life to the full.
A dream with no crying, screaming, killing and death, just a life
                                             of happiness.
This poem is just to say I had a dream.

Matthew Newby (11)
Alcester High School

I Have A Dream

I have a dream
To look after poor people and to let them
Have food and warmth.

I have a dream
To go on a safari and meet all the animals
Especially the elephant.

I have a dream
To own my own cheetah
And to protect the animals in the rainforests.

I have a dream
I would like to see the world,
To have peace, to have happiness wherever we go
I have a dream . . .

Gemma Wadelin (11)
Alcester High School

I Have A Dream

I know the way it should be
All people are meant to be free.

Let's find a solution
To get rid of air pollution.

Do away with coughs and sneezes
Put an end to all diseases.

We need to protect all big cats
Make nothing extinct - not even rats.

Make love not war
Show war the door.

People will be free
To be what they want to be.

And now no one should go hungry
People will live in harmony together in good weather.

We want to keep the forests
And all the animals in them.

That's my dream.

Rosalie Clark (11)
Alcester High School

I Have A Dream

I have a dream, a really good dream
I hear the sound of the ball in the back of the net.
The chanting and screaming of the crowd
I see the reactions of the breathtaking goals.
I feel the breeze drifting off the stadium.
The ball clashing against the boot.
The smell of the warm, refreshing Pukka Pies.
The clapping of the audience.
The rustling of the coats.
I have a dream.

Becky Lee (12)
Alcester High School

I Have A Dream

I dream about the fun I have every night and day
Usually at eleven o'clock I go out and play.
People make discussions of what will happen next, like poverty
and war
But when they think it's stopped another thing happens next.
I have a dream that I could stop this all
By standing up for things and they'd think that I could rule.
We would get along with everyone.
So if you have a different dream, share it with us all
But first you must take this on board.

Chris Hill (11)
Alcester High School

I Have A Dream

I have a dream
A dream of all dreams
To own my own pony
Oh if only.

Day after day
I wish and I wish
That my dream would come true
To own my own pony.

Then one day to my surprise
I could not believe my eyes
A beautiful bay
Stood eating hay.

We gallop through fields
Jump over stiles
But on my bottom I land
With a broken hand.

Oh what a dream!

Amelia Hopkins
Alcester High School

I Have A Dream

I have a dream
Where war is no more,
And the world is perfect
Right to the core.

I have a dream
Where there's no such thing
As greed
Or even obsession with bling!

I have a dream
Where people are treated the same
Whether they are black or white
Or entirely insane.

I have a dream
Where poverty is out of sight
And we can help the Africans
See a colossal ray of light.

I have a dream
Where global warming vanished
And everything's perfect
Spit, rubbed and polished.

And
If we could make this last
We really could have a blast!

Philippa Buxton (12)
Alcester High School

I Have A Dream

We all have dreams, but do they come true?
Because I have a dream . . .
I have a dream that the world's full of love
And no one suffers or feels pain, that's my dream.

We all have dreams, but do they come true?
Because I have a dream . . .
I have a dream that we'll win the cup final
And I'll go down in history, that's my dream.

We all have dreams, but do they come true?
Because I have a dream . . .
I have a dream that they'll get back together
My mum and dad won't fight anymore, that's my dream.

Dreams do come true because we've won the cup final
And my mom and dad are back together
Although we're still waiting for the world to be full of love
I suppose we always will.

Yasmin Murphy (11)
Alcester High School

I Had A Dream

I had a dream that everything was free,
That nothing was locked up,
Nothing was kept for our own pleasure.

I had a dream that people weren't nasty to animals,
People weren't greedy for more of them,
And nobody abused them for any reason.

I had a dream that zoos weren't greedy,
And people were smart enough to stop them
So who is to blame?

Lots of people have animals locked up
Why? Is what I say!
People have no right to say who gets what.
So please stop this madness
Let them be free!

Sam Precious (11)
Alcester High School

I Had A Dream

I had a dream
To help the world
Start a team
Stop famine maybe.

Ethiopia that's my target
Not just a trip to the market
Raise some money like Live Eight
And send the donations in a huge crate.

Freedom and rights for all
Martin Luther King, great man was he
Protested and stood up against white men
Now they are free.

Bono or Geldof that's who I want to be
Schools, hospitals for all
So they are educated and can have a ball
Now let's see how life's meant to be.

Look at the past
What do you see?
Their memories shall last
Make the difference today like they did.

Alex Frost-Head (12)
Alcester High School

I Have A Dream

I have a dream
I can fly up to the sky
Up in the clouds fluffy and white
Next to the sun, big, yellow and bright
Up in the clouds
Look what I can see
No worries in the world
What a great place to be.

Jordan Clarke (12)
Alcester High School

I Have A Dream

I have a dream
A dream that no one else has but me.

I dream I'm a dolphin
Deep down in the bottom of the sea.

I see the sea is calm
No myth, no charm.

I see a gentle wave go by
And as it goes I look up at the big blue sky.

I poke my head up for a second or two
And what's that I see? I haven't got a clue.

It's shining in the blue sky
It's so big and so high.

It twinkles like a butterfly
So big and so shy.

Such a beautiful thing makes the world so fun
I wonder what it is.

Could it be, how could it be?
I think, just maybe it's the sun.

Lauren Townsend (11)
Alcester High School

I Have A Dream

I have a dream of peace throughout the world,
Where aggression will never be seen
All starving will cease, no need for police
Crime will vanish (Maybe I'll learn Spanish)
All joking apart
Before long we will be choking our hearts
Germs and fertilized food
Sickness and health is rude
That makes the world change its mood.

Liam Beck (11)
Alcester High School

I Have A Dream

They say I'm just a daydreamer
Dreaming my whole life through
Chasing after rainbows that will never come true.

Today I saw a dreamboat
He was a vision in blue
Electric smile
Sparkling eyes too.

They say that if you really want it
Dreams can come true
I'm gong to keep my fingers crossed and hope that's true.

Charlie Stanley (12)
Alcester High School

Litter

All the rubbish filling up the streets
From other people's pop and sweets,
They don't care about the litter-picking man
They throw their rubbish wherever they can.

The litter bug that haunts our streets
Bin the rubbish from your sweets,
Paper and bags never in the bins
Bin your rubbish, it's not a sin.

People throwing litter every day
It's not magically going to go away,
Don't throw your rubbish on the floor
Just for the other people to ignore.

In the town, it's all around
McDonalds, KFCs all over the ground,
Put your rubbish in the bin
Keep the streets tidy, just drop it in.

Throwing it from the car without a care
Then carrying on as if it's not there,
Cans, tins, sweet wrappers, the lot
All being left on the ground to rot.

Don't drop the litter from what you've just bought
Stop and give it another thought,
Because the traffic warden is wandering the town
Ready to fine you fifty pound!

People throwing rubbish like wild
Not thinking that they are harming a child,
Or maybe even an innocent duck
Just coming over to have a look.

All the rubbish flying around with the wind
Pick up your rubbish, it should have been binned!

Bethaney Smith (13)
Alderman Smith School

I Have A Dream

I have a dream
That my children and, in turn, their children
Will grow up into a world
Where war is no more
And poverty is gone.

Wars keep going on with real reasons undercover
There seems to be no love, it's like brother hates brother
Young soldiers sent to war being forced to leave their mothers
But wars are only caused by not trusting or respecting each other.

People are killing and people are dying
Evil keeps triumphing over good, but the good keep on trying
They seem to have no luck, only end up sighing
But these wars would stop if the government stopped lying!

There's ongoing suffering and the youth die young
Poor people could have a feast, oh what a rich man just sung
Some people would give anything to taste the taste on their tongue!

People are starving they have nothing to eat
They would rejoice at the sight of a small scrap of meat
They would leap with excitement if taken to a leat
Because they don't have anything, hardly any clothes or sandals
                                                                        for their feet.

Laura Watkins (12)
Alderman Smith School

I Have A Dream

I have a dream
Money isn't important,
We all live quite happily
Not trying to compete.

We never used to have lots
So why now the change?
No designer, no labels
Or stuff with brand names.

I have a dream
Money isn't important
We all live quite happily
Not trying to compete.

People don't realise the causes
Bullying, arguing and violence
Or even plastic surgery
Well, for the people with pence.

I have a dream
Money isn't important
We all live happily
Not trying to compete!

Demi Ashby (13)
Alderman Smith School

I Have A Dream

I would love to see the world change to a better place
By throwing all the criminals all the way to space.

There wouldn't be any murderers or people who shoot a gun
It's not fair on other people, come on, it's not fun.

My dream involves making the world poverty free
But I do wish everyone would follow me.

There would be no more shoplifters,
No more pain and no more bombers on the London trains.

So that's my dream, I hope it comes true
To make the world safe for me and for you.

Sophie Downes (13)
Alderman Smith School

I Have A Dream

I wish I could make the world a better place,
Happy people and a smiling face,
A world I'd like to see.

A world of love and understanding,
No more hunger, war or suffering,
A world I'd like to see.

I would make poor and rich equal,
And make no homeless people,
A world I'd like to see.

Stop racism, it's not a game,
Black or white, we're all the same,
A world I'd like to see.

I guess you could say it's only make-believe!

James Sidwell (13)
Alderman Smith School

I Have A Dream

I have a dream to be a professional horserider,
To win the Grand National or even to win a fiver.
Me and my horse would win them all,
Then we would go home and have a ball.
The very next day we would go again,
I would saddle her up come snow or rain.
It was time to give her a day off,
So I gave her a bath, she's such a show-off.
So that's my dream, I hope it comes true,
I'll be in touch soon with a rosette or two.

Eliesha Galland (13)
Alderman Smith School

I Have A Dream

Money is such an important thing
But happiness it cannot bring.
It will buy you clothes and buy you food
Which may slightly improve your mood.
But it can never ever compare
To the love of a person who will always be there.
Which is why it's ever so sad
When people are killed for money they've had.
Which makes you stop and ask yourself
What price do we have to pay for wealth?
Innocent people are ending up dead
Going out on your own, you may dread.
Just walking down a quiet street
Not knowing who you're going to meet.
Why should we put up with this?
Why should lives be put at risk?
I dream that lives should not be lost
With friends and family paying the cost.
I have a dream.
I have a dream.

Laura Timms (13)
Alderman Smith School

My Dream

I would like to be a famous goalkeeper
And play for a famous football team.
To play against Chelsea and Man United
That is my very big dream.

I'm playing in a game and there's ten minutes to go
The score is 2-2 and it's all set for a draw,
When a player is fouled in the box
They have a penalty, a chance to score.

I'm standing in front of the net
Waiting to save the shot,
The player shoots hoping to score
Alas he does not!

The crowd are all cheering
Hip hip hooray
The opponents have not won the match
Because I've saved the day.

Ryan Norman (13)
Alderman Smith School

I Have A Dream

Millions of people have a dream
From ending war to eating ice cream.
Starving children wish for food
Other people wish for things that suit their mood.
I have a different dream
I'd love to be part of the England netball team.
To reach this goal, I'd have to train hard
And even practise shooting in the backyard.
I doubt that my dream will ever come true
But I like having a hobby that I love to do.

Laura Goodenough (13)
Alderman Smith School

I Have A Dream

I have a dream that one day everyone will be happy,
Each person will feel special in their own way,
And everyone treated fairly,
There will be lots of happiness in the world,
With no bullying or pollution,
Everybody will be loved and cared for,
And each person will be kept safe from crimes.
I wish each and every person will be healthy,
And money would not be a big thing in life,
Also houses will be made for the poor and homeless.
I have a dream . . .

Shelly-Ann Gee (13)
Alderman Smith School

I Have A Dream

No moaning or bullying to begin,
'Cause people couldn't buy stuff just in,
Clothes, trainers or computer games,
All that designer gear and the stuff with brand names,
No sale, sale, sale, just the closed shop door,
Poverty, war and suffering no more.

War doesn't happen cos everyone said,
Let's think about things like drink and bread,
No fighting, all that blood and guts,
Just sit and think back, that stuff was nuts.
Knives, guns and bombs, they are no score,
Poverty, war and suffering no more.

No need for doctors or medical teams,
Diseases just things in dreams,
There are no pills or surgeon's knife,
People just love living life,
There's a lot of hard work that we shouldn't ignore
So that poverty, war and suffering are no more.

Craig Wilson (12)
Alderman Smith School

I Had A Dream

Down the streets below
My dream looks so hollow
People come and go
Are they friend or foe?
Smell the fumes in the air
And I know life isn't fair
I want to reach my goal
Do what's in my soul
I want to live life to the max
Unfortunately, there's no map
I need to work really hard
To see the As on that card
Where do I go from here?
I'm full of dread and fear
What will the future hold?
The secret is untold.

Anna Breeze (14)
Alderman Smith School

I Have A Dream

I have a dream
My dream is to be an actress
I will make a film or star in a show
With make-up and a dazzling dress
I will shine and I will glow
Everyone will know my name
You will see me in a newspaper
'Cause I am in a world of fame
I will be a bright new star
I will have deep blue eyes
Like the sea at sunrise
This is my dream
And I hope and pray
It will come true some day.

Judy Coleman (14)
Alderman Smith School

I Have A Dream

The sky was very dark and dreary,
Not a whisper or a soul about,
Pitch-black inside her bright blue bedroom
Like a shadow hanging over her.

She was alone in her huge bedroom
Tucked up in her cosy, comfy bed,
Sleeping silently and peacefully
Like a lion ready to hunt food.

Everybody in the house sleeping
When the grandfather clock strikes midnight,
She jumps bolt upright, panting for breath
Like a cheetah sprinting for his life.

The noise suddenly awakens her
Sweat trickling down her chubby, round face,
Thinking about her delightful dream
Like a time machine travelling back.

She can't believe she has woken up
Out of her exciting but strange dream,
Telling her what the future will hold
Like a crystal ball predicting life.

In the deep woods stands a huge palace
Where she is going to live for life,
The future will bring much happiness
Like Cinderella's fairy tale.

Charlotte Smith (13)
Alderman Smith School

I Have A Dream

I have a dream of freedom.
A place for people to walk free.
A world without pain and suffering.
A place I want to be.

I have a dream of happiness.
A safe place for people to enjoy.
A world without crime and fighting.
A place to look after, not destroy.

I have a dream of equality.
A place where everyone is treated the same.
A world full of fairness.
A place empty of blame.

Daniel Wilson (14)
Alderman Smith School

I Have A Dream

I have a dream
I don't know if it's true,
But when I'm feeling down
It always get me through.

Imagine the world through the mirror
How different would we be to each other?
There'd be no need to fear
All the threats of race here.

Occasionally I escape into the world and wish
Someday I will really exist
And then I realise
We'll never have that bliss
When I look out a window
And see a reality of this.

James Reed (13)
Alderman Smith School

I Have A Dream

I have a dream
For this world makes me want to scream,
Look at you all, so vain
You don't care if anyone else is in pain.

You know deep down you're a nobody.
Who wants to be somebody,
You just sit there and stare
You don't even care.

There are people out there dying
Silently praying and crying.
I want no one to feel any pain
It's such a terrible feeling to gain.

I want to feel his heartbeat next to mine
For that would be divine,
That would be the cure for my soul
I would feel complete, whole.

As much as I'd like to object
This world will never be perfect.

Danielle Palmer (14)
Alderman Smith School

I Have A Dream

I have a dream
It's big and great
I wish that my dream
Would come true.

I would like to have a good job
And be really successful
I would like to be happy
And have everything I want.

I would have a big house
And a really nice car
Loads of money
To be a star.

I would be rich
And love what I do,
I would have loads of fun
With my mates too.

Kim Osmond (14)
Alderman Smith School

I Have A Dream

I have a dream,
To dance and twirl,
Upon a lit-up stage.
I have a dream of fame and fortune,
To be known to all the world,
With flashing cameras
And glitzy costumes
All eyes will be on me!

All eyes will be on me,
When I dance up on the stage
For all the world to see,
With the glitzy costumes and bright lights
Fame and fortune calls for me!

Bianca Hutchinson (14)
Alderman Smith School

I Had A Dream

I had a dream one winter's night,
Of going to Sheffield for a judo fight.
The competitors came from nationwide
I was hoping luck was on my side.
Seven fights I battled through
After each win my confidence grew.
The final came, I felt so bold
With a massive throw, I took gold!
I stood on the podium feeling proud
Hearing cheers and applause from the crowd.
In October in Sheffield my dream came true
I became national champion - one of a few.

James Gallacher (14)
Alderman Smith School

My Dream

Funny world is it not?
Where people seek revenge and plot
But what all the people do not know
Is where all the bullies and terrorists go.
I shall wish they could get cursed
Before another anger outburst.
But what a world it shall be
Without people picking on me!

Alex Rose (11)
Alderman Smith School

I Have A Dream

I have a dream that no one is ever poor
That relationships never end
That no one dies of disease
That everyone has a best friend.

I have a dream that no one gets bullied
Or laughed at for what they do,
I wish there were no fights
So think about what people go through.

I have a dream that everyone is healthy
That nobody is scared to go to school
Because there is always somebody who can help
So you can feel really, really cool.

Joe Gillespie (11)
Alderman Smith School

I Wish

I wish I was an angel
An angel in the sky.

I wish I was a fairy
A fairy which could fly.

I wish I was a flower
A flower that was bright.

I wish I was a butterfly
A butterfly which flew at night.

I wish, I wish, I wish
I wish those things came true.

But a wish is only a wish
That stays between me and you!

Nicole Teagles (12)
Alderman Smith School

Dreams

Dreams, dreams, happy or sad
Dreams, dreams, good or bad.

Dreams are different in many ways
You have different dreams on different days.

Dreams, dreams, laughter or pain
Dreams, dreams, sunny or rain.

Dreams are weird, they might scare you
So freaky, you might wee or poo!

Sophie Bates
Alderman Smith School

I Have A Dream

I have a dream
That the world and I will be safe,
That people don't fight,
That relationships never end
That no one is ever poor.

I have a dream,
That there are no battles,
That all animals are safe,
That no one is ever hurt,
That the old never die.

I have a dream,
That all the old can see their future,
That people can enjoy their life,
That everyone is happy,
That people have food, drink and water.

I have a dream
That everyone keeps safe,
That people watch what they drink,
That people never take drugs,
That everyone gets along.

I have a dream . . .

Alice Blackwell (12)
Alderman Smith School

My Dream

My numbers have come up
I've won the lottery!
I don't know what to do,
I'll just jump with joy and glee.

One million pounds,
That's how much I've won.
A fast car,
Wouldn't that be fun?

Next on the list,
Perhaps a mouse
No, that's stupid,
I'll buy a posh house.

Luxuries we'll have,
I won't be a fool,
Trampolines or snooker,
Or even a swimming pool.

A trip overseas,
To a nice sunny place,
Somewhere exotic,
Will put a smile on my face.

I know I'll have a party,
A foam party is the theme,
All my mates can come,
This is my dream.

Rory Smith (13)
Alderman Smith School

My Dream

I wish I had never watched that movie,
The one with the blood and guts!
The man with the scary face,
And lots of messy cuts!

Mum said I shouldn't have watched it,
I didn't listen of course.
I wish I had now listened,
Because I'm shaking like a horse!

Now I know I will have nightmares,
Bet my life I will.
I wished I hadn't watched that movie,
The one called Blood, Guts And Kill!

My nightmare was terrible,
Same movie, different stars.
I was in the lead role,
The one left with all the scars.

I hate that movie I watched,
I'll never see it again!
I'm scared of everything now,
Even silly things like the rain!

Rachael Lackenby (13)
Alderman Smith School

Dream Poem

I had a dream about world peace
No wars, no fighting
Not even kids on the street
Everyone you met was happy and cheerful
And never dreadful
Everyone was good, not a single person was sad.

Kieren Ball
Alderman Smith School

Dreams

I've dreamt about a thousand things
From sunflowers to daffodils.
I've been a princess then a dragon,
A passionate kiss then a brutal hit.
I know when I awake that nothing is real.
But as soon as I fall asleep
The darkness soon goes,
To being filled with very bright sun.
I'm in a field filled with corn
Can't find my way out as it's too high,
I search and search till I fall
I know when I awake nothing was real!

Ruth Nelmes (14)
Alderman Smith School

My Poem

When I come home I tell my mum,
What kind of day I've had,
It's a very strange story I am going to tell,
All about my schoolday and how it was bad.
First I start with the bullies,
That always hurt me so.
Then I have the teachers
That ask me questions I do not know.
Next there are the name-callers
Who always call me Strange.
I hope that someday
They will change their wicked ways.
They are a threat to the school,
They don't deserve to be cool!

Jonathan Bell
Alderman Smith School

The Captain Of The Titanic

There I was lying in bed
When a dream appeared into my head.
What would it be like to be the captain of the Titanic?
To get away from the noise and the traffic.
This new ship was a sight to see,
I couldn't believe it was going to be captained by me.
The ship set sail,
On a journey not to fail.
Drifting along the Pacific Ocean,
With a swaying motion.
But unaware of what was going to happen,
So I went to my cabin.
And had a rest
In my nest.
I woke to a crash
'There goes my bangers and mash!'
I was eating my tea
When they called for me.
Sirens and alarms all aloud,
I looked out my window and there was a crowd.
I went out to see what had happened,
To see if anything needed a mend.
But I could see it was a mountain of ice,
People were running around like mice.
The ship started to go down,
I had to go down without a frown.
But I woke up before the water could get me,
For I could see
It was only a dream,
Although real it did seem.

Luke Edmond
Alderman Smith School

Dreams Of . . .

I hope that when I go to bed
Nice thoughts and dreams come into my head.

Dreams of chocolate, dreams of love,
Instead of fists and being shoved.

Dreams of make-up and having fun
Instead of being called names, like scum and dumb.

Dreams of burgers, dreams of fries,
Instead they take my dinner money and no one's around to hear
                                                                                my cries.

I'm tired of standing alone in the shadows,
Being scared to death by a bunch of saddos.

Does anyone know, does anyone care
That when I wake it will still be there?
That terrible living nightmare!

Danielle Roper (12)
Alderman Smith School

Untitled

It's really cold, it's raining hard
I have my hood on tight
I'm nearly running down the road
I can hardly see left or right.
There's something over there not moving
What is it I can see?
It's her, the one they said about and she's watching me!
I pretend I haven't noticed and quicken up my pace
I dare to look again, I look all around the place.
A big sigh of relief, she's gone, I rush to tell my mates
I'm almost at the school, oh no, she's there outside the gates.
I go to walk on by her, I lengthen up my stride
And then she's right beside me, I wish I could have died.
I'm shaking not of cold,
'You're next,' she sniggers in my face, 'consider yourself told!'
I stand still right in front of her; I look her in the eye
'I know your reputation but I'm not scared of you,' said I
'Your bullying days are over as far as I'm concerned
No one will stand for it anymore, the tables have been turned!'
I hear a noise, a ringing noise and then I realise
Thank goodness I was dreaming as I opened up my eyes.

Rosie Jones (12)
Alderman Smith School

Bully

Oh no, it's school again today
I wish that I could stay away.
The pain I feel is always there
Even when they just stand and stare.

How can I get my mum to say
'Why don't you stay home today?'
I'd stay in my bed, safe and warm
The only place away from the storm.

I walk in the gates and find a place to hide
Pray for bell so I am safe inside.
The teacher looks at me and says,
'You look so unhappy these days.'

Give me the strength to speak out loud
So I can come out of this black cloud.
School should be happy, safe and fun,
But all I want to do is run.

Thomas Compton (12)
Alderman Smith School

The Bullied Dream

Far away I drift to sleep
While in the distance someone weeps.
I hear a cry
Throughout the night.
A distant moaning,
Then a fright.
I wake up shocked,
To my surprise,
I see a person say, 'Close your eyes.'
I close my eyes to see
A poor young person just like me.
A great big bully stood there smirking,
While hurting a child. What is lurking?
Around the corner, to my shock,
Is Mother in her cooking frock.
I stand there crying with bad cuts,
What could I do with those horrid looks?
Though what I saw through my tender eyes,
A warm happiness broke out inside.
I woke up nice to my surprise
Back in my home it felt nice.
I went to school and stood up tall
I saw the bully who hurt them all.
'Not to worry, my dear friends
Today he's driven round the bend.'
On that night I went to sleep,
Calm, peaceful and very neat.
At least I'm home, home at last
I know I won't get a blast
Of that bully down the road.

Sophie McGee (11)
Alderman Smith School

Untitled

D reams and thoughts go through my head
R ainbows, dragons, adventures are said
E xciting and frightening I don't mind
A ll night long I wish to find
M emories, stories, people and places
S miling, cheering or unhappy faces.

Daniel Southworth (12)
Alderman Smith School

If I Had A Wish

If I had a wish my wish would be
That everyone would live happily.
The world could be a better place
And everyone with a smile on their face.

If I had a wish my wish would be
Some days would be better for me.
I'm glad me and my friends are there for each other
In times of trouble we help one another.

Emma Higgins (12)
Alderman Smith School

I've Had A Dream

I've had a dream
Where no weapons of destruction were being made
Where world hunger wasn't true
Where illness wasn't too
Everything was perfect, nothing wrong
Then destruction came along.
It's hit here, it's hit there
Soon it'll hit everywhere.

Jake Ryland (12)
Alderman Smith School

Dreams

Everybody has dreams,
Good ones, bad ones,
Happy ones, sad ones,
Everybody has dreams!

Your head touches the pillow and you swiftly drift off,
Into a world completely your own.
Be a football player or fly in the high skies,
In the comfort of your very own home!

You could have a nightmare that scares you to death
And you wake up in such a state
You're all dolled up to meet Robbie
And you end up being late!

You may see into the future
What's going to happen the next day
The new people you're going to meet
Or the embarrassing things you might say!

Everybody has dreams,
Good ones, bad ones,
Happy ones, sad ones,
Everybody has dreams!

Ellie Alexander (14)
Alderman Smith School

A Dream

I have a dream
No, I have a nightmare,
An entity of horror has forced its way into my head.

It chases me through endless corridors of night,
My adrenaline is pumping,
My heart is pounding.

My feet lead me through doors I don't wish to enter,
The pain in my legs is too much,
I begin to slow.

The creature gains ground,
And the bile begins to rise in my throat,
I sprint but I know it is not enough.

I close my eyes as the monster approaches,
I scream as its hands wrap around my throat,
Suddenly, nothing, not a whisper.

The beast is gone,
There is no chill in my bones,
I open my eyes and discover I am home, safe.
A nightmare!

Sorrin Parsons (14)
Alderman Smith School

Dream

When I went to sleep last night,
I had a wonderful dream.
It wasn't one that gave you a fright,
It was one that made you gleam.

I dreamt that I was a famous singer,
As I sat down and peered.
I didn't know whether to go or linger
Until people cheered.

I stood up on stage and sang my best,
I could hear the roar of the crowd.
I could feel my heart beat in my chest
As I started to feel proud.

After the show I was really happy
It felt like I was floating.
My manager was really snappy
Because I couldn't stop gloating.

When I woke up I was a bit upset,
Because the fantasy had ended,
That dream last night I'll never forget
But my day was better than intended.

Holly Carpenter (14)
Alderman Smith School

Bully

I was walking and I froze
There they were.
Looking, staring, waiting.
They came up and pushed me,
It was all over, my dream
I was running and I fell
There they stood
Grinning, smiling, ready to fight.
They came up and pushed me,
It was all over, my dream
My dream! My dream!
I was hopping, I tripped,
There they crouched,
Watching, hoping, shaking their heads,
They came up and pushed me,
It was all over, my life
My life!

Nenagh Brady (11)
Alderman Smith School

I Have A Dream

I have a dream
Of a starry night
But it's not as it seems
You may get a fright
That suddenly clouds appear
And the rain starts to fall
So I start to look
Here
There
Everywhere
Until I find it
This is what I was looking for
The battlefield where my dad fought
He survived to say goodbye
I don't know why
He could have died right there
He did tell me to beware
To never go to war
I know he's right
And in the night
When I'm asleep
I have a dream
That my dad is alive
And war didn't survive.

Kyle Ryland (14)
Alderman Smith School

Dreams

Dreams are good,
Dreams are bad,
But sometimes they make you mad.
Dreams are funny,
Dreams are scary,
But sometimes I just dream of fairies.
Some have meanings,
Some do not,
But some we have just forgot.
Children dream,
Night and day,
And they dream while they play.
Playing and riding bikes,
Makes their dreams a delight.
People dream while they sleep,
Some people even dream of sheep
In a field or jumping a gate,
Sometimes it just keeps you awake.
Not all dreams are nice,
Some just give you a fright.
Creepy-crawlies, snakes and things
Will sometimes appear in my dreams.
Dreams are pictures in the mind,
They make you smile
They make you cry
Some dreams are cool
And you wish that you could rule,
A mansion, a castle or a palace.
Some dreams come true,
If you want them to.

Christine Briggs (11)
Alderman Smith School

I Have A Dream

I have a dream where my family and I have a never-ending life.
When people with a different race get treated like no other.
Because it's the inside that counts.
Where people don't take drugs or hurt others with any sort of violence.
I have a dream where you one day will dream similar things
                                            just like I do.
So don't be scared of a dream.

Guy Griffiths (11)
Alderman Smith School

I Wish, I Wish

I wish, I wish
For a beautiful world
With peace and love all around.

I wish, I wish
For lovely days
Of sun and fun for all around.

I wish, I wish
For joy and happiness
For everyone.

I wish, I wish
For sunny days and rainy nights.

I wish, I wish
There were no bad people
So everyone feels safe.

I wish, I wish
There's plenty of food
For everyone to eat.

I wish, I wish
For a friend in deed
To be there when I need.

Nicole Baskett
Alderman Smith School

In My Fantasy Dream

When I go to sleep at night
First I must turn out the light
Then I lie upon my bed
On my pillow I rest my head.

As the music starts and dreams begin
I dance on my toes to a violin
I swirl and twirl like a storm
Then suddenly my outfit's torn.

Then the hip-hop beat kicks in
I click my boots and make a din
I dance around on the glittery stage
The crowd begins to jump in rage.

The music spins and faces glow
The other dancers shout, 'Go girl go!'
Dance quicker, quicker, spin then jump
I dance so fast my heart goes *thump!*

The music slows and quietly dies
My super dream is a pack of lies
My quilt's in knots my pillow's gone
Do you know if I danced anyone?

I go downstairs and tell the world
I danced, I spun, I twinkled and swirled
In my fantasy dream.

Bayli Jones
Alderman Smith School

Dream

When I dream
They're so extreme.
Winter, spring, summer, autumn
Once dreamed I'd bought them.
I like having fun,
Especially in the sun.
Dreaming is the best
I could just sit and rest.
I wish I could dream all the time
'Cause when I dream I'm just fine.
This is the end of the dream
Or so it would seem.

Natasha Wickett (11)
Alderman Smith School

I Have A Dream

I have a dream
For people to judge people for who they are
To stop bullying
For people to appreciate what other people do.

I have a dream
To give people shelter
To give people drink and food.

I have a dream
For people to not solve things by fighting
And to be friends instead.

Bethany Marshall (12)
Alderman Smith School

Mr Rossborough

I respect him for the way he talks,
Never have I heard him raise his voice,
As chilled as the Arctic
So tall like a tree,
He is the type of role model people would like to be.

We've had our ups and downs,
We've also seen some frowns,
With parents coming in and out,
It's almost like a roundabout.

He's kind and caring,
He likes using words like *tilth*.

He is a percipient young man,
And he finds out all he can.
He is as consistent as a prism
And loves all of that existentialism.

Zara Mohammed (15)
Ashlawn School

My Mum

My mum is the best
She beats all the rest
She is so beautiful
She makes me happy
She makes me smile.

My mum does everything for me
And I love her for that.
When she's cross, I find it funny
But she's just too nice.
But I just do as she says
To make her happy.

My mum spoils me
I think I am too spoilt sometimes,
She is always buying me new clothes
She seems to like buying me things
Even if it's my dad's money
Which I find quite funny.

Nicole Hutchinson (14)
Ashlawn School

I've Only Got You

I want to let you know that I love you.
You're so beautiful, girl, let me get it on,
I want to take care of you because I've never done you wrong.
Oh, girl, I've loved you for life and I really mean that,
You're so special to me, I want to keep that.
From the moment we met I hit you like a clip,
I am not lying because I like your stitch,
With your long black hair and baby-blue eyes
I'm coming for you, so get your nature rise.
I hear you calling my name but you haven't got to wait
I'm always thinking of you because you're my soulmate.
I love the way you put your hand on my chest whilst you kiss it softly,
Shorty, you're the best; it's plain to see that you were meant for me.
I'll give you everything you need, so no need to stress.
Girl, I want to tell you all about my feelings,
I want to get close to my heart that I was stealing
To finally make you so appealing.

Muneeb-Ur-Rahman Saharan (14)
Ashlawn School

Thierry Henry

He wears the number 14 and he plays up front,
As he gets the ball his first touch is immaculate.
His pace threatens the defenders
He dribbles past 1 and then 2,
There is only one defender left, what's he going to do?
A couple of step-overs and a couple of kick-ups
The defender panics and takes him out.
Henry, a free kick, wizard, alla-ka-zam and the ball is at the back
of the net.
Take a bow Thierry Henry!

Karanjit Virk (15)
Ashlawn School

Parents

Everything I know and everything I do is affected by my parents
And what they choose to do.
They influence my life, though they do make me wash up.
Everything I own and everything I use is bought through my parents
Because I'm too cheap myself.
They influence my income and don't make me pay rent.
Everything I am and everything I will be is affected by my parents
And what they do for me.
They influence who I am and what I do for them.

Andrew Oldroyd (14)
Ashlawn School

Martin Johnson

The alpha male of the old England pack
Rucking and mauling on the attack.
Standing up tall with blood on his shirt
Running and sliding on rugby pitch dirt.
With ball in his hand he is the best
As the English rose beams on his chest.
French, Irish and the Welsh too
Have no idea what this man can do.
Like a tank he grinds up the wet pitch
His boots stuck firmly into a ditch.
The stadium crowd shouts out his name
As him and his boys win yet again.
Focused and thinking on what to do next
On the training pitch move, put into context.
Now the big game is here to play
England, Australia, Cup Final day.
The trophy is gleaming a super gold
After this game, it's his to hold.
For the first time in history
He led England to World Cup victory.
Martin Johnson is a true hero
And will be remembered wherever he goes!

Liam Bailey (15)
Ashlawn School

She

She is like no other
She is the stars at night and the moon so bright
When she is near, the rain is clear
And the sun smiles like she.

She's had it tough
But that's not enough
She won't stop or drop
Because a saint is she.

The people she loves
Always come first
In her life of hustle and bustle
She's always on the go
And never lolls about the lounge.

She beams on life
Like a butterfly at its highest point
She is my life
She is my mum.

Jessica Holton (15)
Ashlawn School

Inspiration

Bob Geldof had an idea
To give Africa new life,
He wanted to relieve it
From its struggle and its strife.

So he got some famous bands to play
On a multicoloured stage,
People flocked from everywhere
Saw the dawn of this new age.

We all clicked our fingers as a sign
Of the sadness that must stop,
But in the same week something happened
That made our love and caring drop.

Bombs had wiped away the caring
Death had wiped away the love,
What had made the inspiration
Fly away, just like a dove?

We don't think how to make goodness
From the loathing and the hate,
So why do we give up on dreams
To sit around and wait?

Now no one thinks of our idea
To give Africa new life
No one thinks how to relieve it
From its struggles and its strife.

Victoria Taylor (15)
Ashlawn School

My Inspiration

Inspiration is not to be taken lightly,
It takes a very special person to do,
They must be an amazing individual,
To inspire someone like you.

Inspiration can make you do many different things,
It can make you work hard, aim high,
And capture the feelings it brings.

My grandma is my inspiration,
She makes me happy when I am sad,
She inspires me to fulfil my life
With the wonderful things she had.

One day I hope I will inspire
Someone just like me.
I will work extremely hard
To help them see all the things they wish to see.

Sally Whitmore (15)
Ashlawn School

Ronaldo, Who Wears Number 7

Ronaldo, he wears number 7
When he dies he'll go up to Heaven
He dances on the ball
That looks really cool
It's Ronaldo who wears number 7.

Ronaldo, he wears number 7
He's in Ferguson's top eleven
He's only just eighteen
But he still makes the team
It's Ronaldo who wears number 7.

Ronaldo, he wears number 7
A Jaguar, yes, he has driven
He comes from Portugal
When he charges it's like a bull
It's Ronaldo who wears number 7.

Ronaldo, he wears number 7
He likes to go down to Devon
He gets quite a lot of pay
Infact it's way over £10K
It's Ronaldo who wears number 7.

Ronaldo, he wears number 7
He owns a Rottweiler called Treffon
He is my big inspiration
He always stays in formation
It's Ronaldo who wears number 7.

Ronaldo, he wears number 7
He should have been in Ocean's Eleven
He is very skilled
He likes his wine chilled
It's Ronaldo who wears number 7.

James Green (14)
Ashlawn School

The Poem About My Chum

Jenni, Jenni
You are so cool,
Especially when we act like fools.

Jenni, Jenni
You're in a good mood
I cooked at your house and we burnt the food!

Jenni, Jenni
You are quick on the news
You go to New Look and wear dodgy shoes.

Jenni, Jenni
I am a pain
We love Birmingham, let's go on the train.

Jenni, Jenni
You ride a mini moto
We crammed into a booth to get a photo.

Jenni, Jenni
You're my best chum
Town on Saturday, you should come!

Jenni, Jenni
In Neverland we'll feed the horse
If it kills me call Inspector Morse.

Jenni, Jenni
People think we're freaks
In actual fact we're just pure geeks.

Jenni, Jenni
In India we ate goulash
But I know you preferred my bowl of moolash!

James Priest (15)
Ashlawn School

The Muse

Dear, you are my muse
My creative heart beats within your chest
Slowly rising and falling

Please don't cry dear
I couldn't bear to lose the spark
The muse

Now the ink has been spilled
The paper is sodden
Blue blood seeps into every crevice of the crisp paper
It spreads like butter
Your feet tread the path
The spilled ink squelches under your feet

You inspire me to write this poem
You knocked over my ink well
You made the paper sodden
And made the blue blood run

Dear, you are my muse
And forever will be.

Antony Lowe (15)
Ashlawn School

The Man Who Invented Football

The man who invented football
He must have been really clever,
He didn't have a football shirt
Or any clothes whatsoever.

The man who invented football
He didn't even have a ball,
Or boots, or shinpads or anything like that
They used a skull, that's all.

The cave mouth was the goal mouth
The wind was the referee,
When the man who did it, did it
In 30,000 BC.

The man who invented football
Was an inspiration to me,
He couldn't have been a woman
He must have been a he!

The man who invented football
If he were here today,
He'd probably get a knighthood
Hip hip hooray!

Jake Rugman (14)
Ashlawn School

Inspiration

Inspiration can be shown in many different ways
It could be a peaceful countryside or a roadside cafe
A sweet little girl or a sexy city stripper
A respectful vicar or a lonesome drug dealer
There's always a place for inspiration
And there's always a place in your heart for it.

To inspire, is to motivate the body into something great
And it's something in your life that you cannot live without.
My inspiration is so far away but yet I believe in it
A relation of mine that inspired me with confidence
Had faced the greatest stage of his life.
To go on a battlefield with a gun and be surrounded by the enemy
Not knowing whether you would survive the dreadful night.
The friends he made and the friends he lost,
To be courageous in a scene like that
Deserves a medal in his brave life.
Hearing screams turn to silence
And watching life turn to death.
To watch a bullet slash through his mate's head
And escape through the other side.
To see men kneel to the ground in pain
Nothing can be compared to the patriotic assignment they led.
To fight for your country is one man's dream,
To die in battle is one man's nightmare.
Once he fought the horrific battle
The man I once knew was totally changed.
If I was to be inspired to achieve something
I will always remember that man that bravely once lived.

Tom Pinks (14)
Ashlawn School

A Whole New World

No one alone
No one suffering
No more hunger
No more war.

Just stop and think
Just for one second
What would you change?
What changes to the world?

No one alone
No one suffering
No more hunger
No more war.

I know what I would change
Not money, not life
Well, other's lives
So no more hunger or suffering or war

No one alone
No one suffering
I'd like to think
That one day
It will change.

Rebecca Dandy (12)
Ashlawn School

Heart And Desire

My heart's on fire,
My zip's up tight,
I'll hold your hand every night,
My heart and desire is on fire.

I'll be with you every night,
Don't let go with any fright,
Don't take a step or let go,
I'll be with you from head to toe.

Just remember friendship never ends,
That's why I have all of my friends.

Tiffany-Jade Jones & Leia-Summer Jones (11)
Ashlawn School

Inspiration

Everyone needs inspiration
Is it to do with globalisation?
Many people have a desire
It sets them off like a spark of fire
It's that thing that sets your heart beating
It's about fun, not cheating
It's like a leaf, get a grip or it might fly away
It all happens on this particular day.

Many people inspire me
People like Kylie
I like to inspire
I like to escape from reality divided by a fence of wire
I feel so happy with a pen and a book
This is my poem, take a look
It's like a leaf, get a grip or it might fly away
It all happens on this particular day.

Think of rhyme, rhythm and beat
Make up lyrics, it will sound sweet
So next time you make up a rhyme
Save the lyrics from their death bell chimes
And remember you are a poet
And you know it
It's like a leaf, get a grip or it might fly away
It all happened on this particular day.

Meg Cahill (11)
Ashlawn School

Inspiration

The idea of inspiration
To be inspired by an icon
Gaining ideas from the great
Is not imagination.

The idols of the ages
Ignite in us a feeling
Of such powerful desire
It truly is amazing.

When you have an idea
That's nearly out of reach
Inspiration pulls you on
There's nothing like it.

The creative force
The influence
You cannot understand
The power to inspire
Is now yours to command.

David Hooker (15)
Ashlawn School

Thierry Henry

The glory and power of red
No more need be said.
The tricks performed by number fourteen
Make him the best in the team.
Speed and skills lead to victory
And bring home to Highbury a trophy.

Now he has to fulfil his role
The match is down to this goal.
With burning desire
Passion and fire
The ball hits the back of the net!

We have won the Champions League
Our players are tired with fatigue.
The fans are not done
With pride they run
To the pitch and in triumphant unison they say
Arsenal!

Priyan Mistry (14)
Ashlawn School

My Mum Is My Mummy

I won't call my mum, Mum
I'll call my mum, Mummy
My mum is mum
Cos I came from her tummy.

She guides me through life
She helps me to strive
It's all thanks to her
That I am alive.

I've been through bad times
And she's always been there
I go to her first
Cos I know that she'll care.

Whenever I cry
She's there by my side
If I need a new outfit
She'll help me decide.

If I need a lift
She'll always say fine
And it's small things like this
Why I think she's divine.

She's hip, she's styling
She's so much fun
And although she is blonde
She's really not dumb!

She's special, she's smart
And ever so clever
Would I want to be her?
I'd never say never!

Zöe Baines (15)
Ashlawn School

The Best Friend Poem

James, James
You're so cool
Even though you are a fool.
For you I rate
As my best mate.
You make me laugh
Even though you need a bath.
For me you're always there
And to you I swear
That we are buds puds for life.
James, James
You remember when we burnt that food?
Yeah, you're a dude.
We still need to go to Neverland,
Let's start a new band.
We should never grow up
We're gonna win the World Cup!
We're gonna make jet pack shoes and sing this rhyme all the time,
'You'll be flying in the air with these
Jet packs that you wear
You can fly past Tony Blair
And give him a quick flick of his hair.'
Because we're idiots like that
Remember when I hit you with the rubber bat?
Yeah, we're geeks for life
With no strife,
You're the cat's pyjamas and the bee's knees.

Jenni Wareing (14)
Ashlawn School

Inspiration

Is inspiration what we can be?
Or is inspiration something we see?
Or is it something that you do?
Who is it that inspires you?

Friends, family, celebrities
It can be whoever you please
The woman who lives next door
The kids who live on the top floor

Is it a close friend, a charity
Or someone that you never see?
Where does inspiration dwell
A funny joke, a brand new smell?

Something you eat with your tea?
Inspiration doesn't cost, it's completely free
Is it what stops us feeling blue?
What does inspiration mean to you?

Michael Judd (15)
Ashlawn School

Keith Moon - My Inspiration

When Keith Moon sat behind his drum kit
Entire rooms full of people would fall silent
The way he played
Was like no other man.

Parapet, parapet, as his sticks hit the snare
He played like a madman
He didn't care.

The facial expression which he acquired
Is that which makes me and many others inspired.

His head flying about,
Like nothing I've seen,
He played with such effort,
He was living his dream.

How his drum kit would shine,
Like a polished diamond,
It was so cool,
I wish it was mine.

But he has left us now,
For a better place,
May he now drums in Heaven
With such power and grace.

Harry Elwell (14)
Ashlawn School

Inspiration

Inspiration? What does it mean to you?
Is it something you see
Or something you do?

Is it the one true voice in the silence?
One suggestion, an opinion
On how to control uncontrollable violence?

Was it the writer of something controversial?
So when he's buried beneath green, green grass
In one hundred years his words are universal

Is the seed beneath the stone
Ever going to know what it's like
To poke its head into the great unknown?

Is it the man locked up in the dark?
He holds a strong belief
That the black, the white, around they would lark.

Is it the man who embraces the diseased?
He wants them to have a happy ever after
And for heavenly justice he would plead.

Is it the suffering mother
Who, those greatest to her are drowned
But she still breaks her back helping another?

Is it the atheist
And despite their differences
He's great friends with a Catholic priest?

Is inspiration the child who faces fear
With the strength only a god could possess
And he never spills a single tear?

Inspiration? What does it mean to you?
Is it something you see
Or something you do?

Catherine Clements (14)
Ashlawn School

Inspiration

All his life he was disrespected
He has been bad and even arrested
But he made his way through
By shocking me and you
With his crazy tunes and blasting his critics to the moon.

He started off in '99
When nothing in life was going fine
He threw down some rhymes
Of a different kind
And his talents started to shine.

His first song came out and without a doubt
He was the most outrageous artist about
The parents cried and cried and cried
About the artist who didn't abide
To the rules of music and lyrical rhyme.

His albums, he made three more
His show, his Curtain Call and Encore
But it wouldn't last long
As age came on
And now he makes music no more.

His career was at its end
Though he still had many friends
He went round the bend
Broke his writing pen
How silly of Eminem.

Josh Cox (15)
Ashlawn School

Zinedine Zidane

Trick stars of them all
Captain leads a great example to them all
The World Cup winner
Zinedine Zidane, the world's best player.

Bags of tricks and skills
Skins up the keeps and kills
Puts the balls into back of the nets
Everyone follows the example that he sets.

Best player in history
Leaves the opposite team in misery
There is no end to pleasing the fans
As they cheer out Zinedine Zidane!

Patrick Mathy (15)
Ashlawn School

Shakespeare Inspiration

'To be or not to be' are well known words
But the creator's name is rarely heard.
William Shakespeare is the man
But he never had any real fans.
He's written so many plays that have been shown
And not once really did he get a moan.
So many look up to old dead Willy
Even Jane, Lucy, me and Billy.
He may be long gone dead
But his lines, by so many, are still said.
I have performed and read
Even though he is stone-cold dead.
He still watches his play alive and well
And has made a life by living out of Hell.

Katy Griffiths (15)
Ashlawn School

Inspiration

Inspiration is what you want it to be
Something you touch, hear or see.
A creative force to influence your life
When you're most at strife.
When everything seems against your heart
Inspiration will help to play its part.
Let these ideas take your mind away
To another world on another day.
Do you use these thoughts for bad or good?
To hurt or help, do what you should.
Will you choose the path of a sinner
Or use them to become a winner?
Inspiration can be a walk on the coast
So what kind of things inspire you most?

Charley Picken (15)
Ashlawn School

Inspiration

Inspiration is in everyone's life
Whether you realise it or not.
It is not until you are in strife
Do you aspire to what is to be got.

There's an influence in everyone's mind
Ruling the part in which dreams are created
It is in their life that they will find
Inspiration in ideas that have been tainted.

It is those that you may envy
Historical figures or your mum
Envy could sting you like poison ivy
It's become jealousy, inspiration is gone.

Deepika Govind (14)
Ashlawn School

Friends

Friends are there when times are rough
And stand by your side when things get tough.
They pick you up when you are down
With a smile but never a frown.
We go on massive shopping sprees
And go to a café for afternoon teas.
We always love to have a laugh
And moan about how we hate maths.
We try on shoes and eat lots of choc
Time flies by as we look at the clock.
I love my girls 'cause they all care
Our favourite game is truth or dare.
We have so much fun talking about boys
But then we decided they make too much noise.
We talk about which one is hot
But then stick to the common lot.
I get so hyper when mates sleep over
When we can drive we'll all to go Dover.
When we're at school we have such a laugh
Most of the time it's about the staff.
We talk about soaps that are on the TV
But we hated our jabs, especially TB.
I treasure my friendships; they'll stay in my heart
I knew I would love them right from the start.
So that's where we are right up to this day
My mates are all wicked, what more can I say.

Sophie McNaughton (15)
Ashlawn School

Eighteen Strings, One Big Character!

A soulful character
Hiding beneath your hair
But who is it that's really there?
You tell your story
For those who listen,
But in your mind, it's all so distant.
You switch off like you have no care,
With all your people standing there.
You quote those words so close to you
So close to all those others too.
You wrote those words to inspire,
For yours and others' own desire.
They inspire me,
They inspire you,
They inspire all those others too.

Hannah Beynon (15)
Ashlawn School

Sunshine In Cyprus

I rest and relax in your warm, hot sunshine
N o more raindrops, just soft sand that is so fine
S un shining brightly as we eat lots of peaches
P eople sunbathing on your soft sandy beaches
I ce creams in all different flavours eaten by everyone
R arely anyone frowns as we melt away in your sun
A lways giving us an exciting holiday that we will remember
T ogether we all have fun on our holiday in September
I t's my favourite place in the world to be
O nce or twice I've been but still some things to see
N ow and again I wish I was relaxing in the sunshine in Cyprus.

Emma Grant (15)
Ashlawn School

My Inspiration

There's only one lesson I truly enjoy
One where the teacher frightens all the boys.
She's interesting, clever and will never judge you,
When life gets you down, she's the one to go to.
She's always wears a smile, which brings a cheerful vibe
When you feel alone and want to hide.
She always makes you feel like you belong
You always wish her lessons were long.
Her opinion makes you think
And she will never make you want to shrink.
Mrs Garratt is my inspiration because she makes me think
One day I want to be just like her.

Kayleigh Phillips (15)
Ashlawn School

Inspirational Figures, Places

The prison room, all floors echo to the beat
The shadow forms of long-gone feet
Its occupant has gone to meet
His freedom.

These bare walls once held
A terrorist? An activist?
Who for his hazy crimes was found
Guilty.

Was it just? Was it fair?
What is just? What is fair?
In white South Africa
No one cared.

Since his release the law has changed
Dominance, repression, suffrage for all.
The rally cry was heard
Many took up his call.

Apartheid ends
Without more blood
South Africa
United.

Now he's old
The victories won,
More mountains to climb
For Mandela.

David Railton (14)
Ashlawn School

I Had A Dream

My magic carpet is taking me high
Up into the midnight sky
The moon with its shadowy silver light
And the stars like diamonds shining bright
This magic carpet I don't need to steer
And as I twirl I have no fear
My magic carpet comes to a stop
And I'm in a land of sweets and pop
Houses made out of mint chocolate chip
And rivers of milkshake that I can sip
The candyfloss clouds are floating by
And I hear a loud enjoyable sigh
Suddenly my carpet starts to spin
And I hear a loud and noisy din
A thud, a bang, and my eyes open wide
And there I am, lying on my side
I open my mouth and start to scream
And I realise I had a dream

Samantha Richardson (12)
Hartshill School

I Have A Dream

I have a dream I will play for Chelsea
And become rich and wealthy.
I want to kick a ball around a pitch,
Not sit like a tramp in a ditch.

I would want to score a goal
I would try with all my soul.
David Beckham would lose a job
But I would be the one to lead the England squad.

Every night I would have a beer
And sit in front of the TV and cheer,
Then I'd go to bed and dream of a fantasy team.

And it all cause of one guy,
Frank Lampard tells me why
I want to be footie star
And kick my dreams faster than a rocket car.

Luke Watson (11)
Hartshill School

I Have A Dream

I have a dream of equal harmony
Everyone equal, all of us the same
All with parallel opportunities.

I have a dream, non-existent evil
All excellent, all brilliantly bright
The universes will never become death.

I have a dream of a grey stone city
Trouble lurking around every corner,
I hope this dream will never become real.

I have dreams of the future years to come.

Paul Callender (11)
Hartshill School

Dreaming Days

When lazy cats on walls outstretched
When cursed sun beats on land wretched
Far away in the land of nod
Their dreaming days of fuss of cod.

Oh how I'd love to be out there
Without a fuss, without a care.
Instead I'm stuck in school, I'm bored
Where a lazy classmate has just snored.

Dreams to be wild,
Dreams of what could be,
Dreams of the captured,
Dreams of the free.

We all live in peace in the land of sleep,
Those confident, quiet
And those who weep.

My dream I tell to you reader today
Accomplish, I might not
Accomplish them I may.
Those who live in the African rot
For them make poverty, a new not.

Adam King (11)
Hartshill School

I Have A Dream

I have a dream
Floating on cloud nine,
I take a sip from my wine
I see the world all calm and peaceful
It all seems so fine.

Now the wine is wearing off
It doesn't seem enough
To stop the fighting and the war
All the poverty and the poor.
I had a dream.

Charlotte Morewood (13)
Hartshill School

I Had A Dream

What if
There was lots of snow
What if
There was world peace
What if
Aliens came to Earth
What if
There was no racism in the world
What if
You got really rich
What if
There were no illegal drugs
What if
There was no smoking
What if
There was education for all
What if
A meteor came to the world
What if
There was no bullying
What if
You were captain of a team
What if
England won the World Cup
What if
The world ended
What if it was all a dream?

Thomas Kidgell (12)
Hartshill School

My Dream

I have a dream
It is not what it seems
This is what it means.

No racism allowed
No bullying too
No violence as well.

I have a dream
It is not what it seems
This is what it means.

All I want is everyone to get on
Any colour, religion or race
It's not what is on the outside,
It is what is on the inside that counts.

I have a dream
It is not what it seems
This is what it means.

No smoking allowed
No drugs too
The world will be clean.

I have a dream
It is not what it seems
This is what it means.

Have you got a dream?

Beth Thompson (12)
Hartshill School

I Have A Dream

I have a dream
That people will learn to accept one another.
I have a dream
That people will stop hurting one another.
I have a dream
That there is no evil in the world.
I have a dream
That everyone has a place in society.
I have a dream
That there is no discrimination towards each other.
I have a dream
Where I am accepted for who I am.
I have a dream
Where I am equal to the people around me.
I have a dream
Where I am loved.
I have a dream
Where I am happy.
I have a dream
Where my dreams come true.
I have a dream
Where I am treated right.
I have a dream
Where I'm not black and blue.
I have a dream
Where I have someone to love me.
I have a dream
Where I feel alive.
I have a dream
Where I can still look into your eyes.

Danielle Le-Blancq (15)
Hartshill School

I Have A Dream

I have a dream
That everyone is happy.
I have a dream
That everyone feels loved.
I have a dream
That everyone is accepted.
I have a dream
That everyone is equal.
I have a dream
That all wars are stopped.
I have a dream
That there is no racism.
I have a dream
That everyone belongs.
I have a dream
That we are one.
I have a dream
That dreams come true.

Stevie Hughes (15)
Hartshill School

I Have A Dream

I have a dream
Imagine the world to be a successful and beautiful environment,
A peaceful and non-violent society,
No racism or thieves,
No crimes or murders!

I have a dream
The world will be a perfect place to be in
A chance to reflect back on all the good things that happen,
No homeless or cruelty
A place where we can all be happy.

I have a dream
There will be no wars or fighting,
No abuse or bullying,
The world will be at peace!

Alicia Pattinson (14)
Hartshill School

I Have A Dream

'I have a dream,'
Wise words once said
By a man who knew the world was wrong.

'I have a dream.'
He used his head,
And saw there'd been a problem for far too long.

He dreamt of a world where love prevailed,
He dreamt of a world without hate,
He dreamt of a world of equality,
In every country, city and state.

But our world's full of violence,
Our streets full of crime.
Our parks full of rubbish,
Our streets full of grime.
Going out with your friends
If it's dark *don't* walk back.
And this rule is double for you
If you're black.

Racism in the workplace,
Racism in the schools,
Racism in the police
Those who make the rules.

He had a dream
Of a nation united,
No prejudice to break it up.

He had a dream
Of a world full of love
It's time to wake up.

Amy Jones (15)
Hartshill School

I Have A Dream

I have a dream
Where marriage is forever
Where children are with both parents
Not forced to join one side
Where it should be equal.

I have a dream
Where men aren't labelled
For race, religion or their reality
Labels are for products
Not for people.

I have a dream
Where fear isn't dictating
And the law is the law
Where people rule
When they are chosen.

I have a dream
Where our greed
Hasn't destroyed our world
Or ruined homes, changed lives
Because of our greed.

Kyle Hollyman (13)
Hartshill School

I Have A Dream

I have a dream
Like many others
That terrorist's stop
And people live in peace.

I have a dream
Like one-hundred thousand people
That the government finally wakes up
And release the British farmer.

I have a dream
Like millions of others
That country leaders
End all poverty.

I have a dream
Like many others
That global warming stops
And the polar ice caps grow.

I have a dream
Like everyone in Britain
That a political party
Does what they say they are going to do.

I have a dream
Like millions of people
That racism stops
And racially different people can live in peace.

Paul Rowland (13)
Hartshill School

I Have A Dream

I have a dream
And this dream is to become a rugby player
Not an ordinary rugby player, one of the lucky few
To become an England player, that will do.
To please the crowd at the Twickenham stand
I would be so proud and grand.
To watch the ball soar so high
Into the floodlight sky.
To win the World Cup again
To battle through all the pain.
Superstardom, here I come
Watch out world, I'm on the run!

Tom Smitham (13)
Hartshill School

I Have A Dream

I have a dream
To get along in peace,
When someone is wrong to you
Move along like grease.

Racism is pathetic
It's something we all hate,
Just get along with it
No, not this date.

Just think like this
If you had a different cultured husband or wife,
Would you be racist to him or her
Or get along in life?

We stand strong
With an army to fight,
But killing innocent people
Do we have that right?

We have a lot of food
So much to spare,
We should share it with those
Whose bellies are bare.

I have a dream
For this world that we live,
To go to the Third World
And do all we can to give, give, give.

Jason Brown (13)
Hartshill School

I Have A Dream

I have a dream
To work for a fashion magazine,
Be rich, successful and have fun
Work hard, get the magazine done.
Go home to my family,
My husband, my kids and me.

I have a dream
That our country will work
Together as a team.
No racism, bullying or war.
Stop it all, let's make this real
Come on, it's how we all feel.

I have a dream
That the world is not how it seems.
It can't be all that bad
That never again would there be a child sad
I wish we could live in peace and harmony
Is this how we all feel or is it just me?

Chloe Markham (14)
Hartshill School

I Have A Dream

The sun shines bright
And we don't fight
Oh I have a dream.

We're all friends
It never ends
Oh I have a dream.

Where birds fly free
Above the sea
Oh I have a dream.

Old oak trees
Swing in the breeze
Oh I have a dream.

No bombs and guns
Or screws for thumbs
Oh I have a dream.

No black or white
It is in sight
Oh I have a dream.

Rachel Windross (13)
Hartshill School

I Have A Dream

I have a dream
Where I am real,
In a world
Beyond imagination.
I have a job,
Well paid too
In my world
You live forever.
I have a dream
That England is
Peaceful and grand
And no hatred at all.
England, my country
Has no racism
Nor terrorism,
Just peace.
I have a dream
Like for our world
To be better.
No wars at all,
No poverty,
No extremists,
No racism,
Just peace.
I just hope
That one day
This dream
Will someday
Come true.
I have a dream . . .

Ben Storer (14)
Hartshill School

I Have A Dream

Those who sleep under the stars
Dream, wish and hope
Those who lie dehydrated
Dream, wish and hope
Those whose children are dying of starvation
Dream, wish and hope
Those who are suffering abuse
Dream, wish and hope
Those who are singled out because of their heritage
Dream, wish and hope.

I could explain a few more things
But I shall not
I could sit and do nothing
But I shall not
Yet, I could act and do something
And I shall
One day, when my dream comes true
We shall unite as one
Let our dreams run free
Banish all the suffering
And dispose of poverty
But most of all
Most important of all
Bring that special something that we call . . . equality.

Sarah Proctor (14)
Hartshill School

I Have A Dream

Most dreams are self rewarded.
Most include life's aspirations achieved.
Flashy houses and snazzy cars,
You'll have everything you need.
But, my dream is not only for me,
Yet for the people of the world.
This is my chance to say what needs to be done,
And I really need to be heard.
This world we live in is a really nasty place.
It is home to wars, hatred, unfair treatment,
It's really in a state.
You and me both know,
We need to change all this,
To peace and happiness all around,
Now wouldn't that be bliss!
The nightmare we live in is reality,
And this dream seems too good to be true,
But with the help of everyone,
My dream is not impossible to do.

Kelly Perrett (14)
Hartshill School

Would You?

If you could go back in time to save the world
Would you?
If you could help someone in need
Would you?
If it took one person with one speech to change the world
Would you?
If you could end poverty with just a few words
Would you?
If you could save hundreds of lives with a simple idea
Would you?
If you could stop racial abuse in twenty-four hours
Would you?

Martin Luther King changed the world for the better in twenty minutes
Just one man, one speech, one voice
Would you?

Shannen Mantack (14)
Hartshill School

My Dream

I have had dreams
For me and you,
But no more dreams
As they will never come true.

This dream was to stop war,
And to create a useful law!
Stop extreme pain,
And love that we need to gain.

I haven't changed my dreams,
To become a vet,
That is my ultimate dream,
And I will become one I bet!

My dream for the world,
Starts at equality
Even though Martin Luther King started it,
We need to continue and not let it slip.

My friends and I have different views,
My family also think of something new,
But I am sure we all have one thing the same,
It's the dream of a better, safer world which we could gain.

So dream for the best,
Pray for the rest,
And maybe your dreams will come true
And the better world will shine through.

Chelsea Richter (13)
Hartshill School

Why?

Why is it fair to be judged by our skin?
Why is it fair to be judged by our religion?
Why is it fair to be judged by our image?
It's not!
So why do people do it
Why is it fair to be judged by our sexuality?
Why is it fair to be judged buy our personality?
Why is it fair to be judged?
It's not!
So why do people do it?

Danielle Purkis (14)
Hartshill School

Biggie And 2Pac

Biggie and 2Pac changed the world
But now they've been chewed,
They went down Death Row and went with the flow.

We all know they're famous for victory and pride,
Now you've died, so you don't have to hide, just have a good ride.

All the gang, put down our boomerangs, and stand up tall
Don't lean up the wall, otherwise you'll have a great fall.

Gunfights are bad, so go run to your dad
Otherwise you'll get hit in the jaw and taken to the floor
Then arrested if you're caught, then we'll be back to square nought.

David Allison (12)
Hartshill School

Bullying

B is for bullying all through the day
U is for uplifting to bully people
L is for losing your dignity
L is for losing everything
Y is for yell for help
I is for ignorant bullying
N is if no reason at all
G is for gangs to bring the pain.

Ryan Lee (12)
Hartshill School

Who Created War?

Who created war?
Why did they create wars?
What for?
People dying, people crying,
Bullets and bombs flying.
People, soldiers, deathbed awaits them.
Who created war?
Why did they create war?
What for?
People dying, people crying.

Robyn Robinson (12)
Hartshill School

Dream The World A Better Place

B ecause the world has
E aten happiness away
T ime of cheerful stories has become a waste
T he racist abuse has taken up all of the world's time
E ither we love or hate
R ealise the world can be a better place

W hy do the black and white fight?
O h why can't we share the same time in the
R ight way of happiness and joy?
L ove each other
D estroy all racist abuse.

      I dream the world could be like this.

Francesca Harris (11)
Hartshill School

My Dad

My dad lives in Australia
Which is ever so far away,
I let him go, it was his dream
But now I don't see him every day.

Everyone wishes their dream to come true
That's why I let him go,
But I have a dream that my dad will come back
Because I love him so.

My first real dream was to swim with killer whales
But then I let that one slip,
Because when you put them both on the scales
My dad would always tip.

I dream and dream real hard each day
But it hasn't come true as yet,
Maybe one day my dad will say
'Right, I'm ready, I'm set.'

So now you know of my dream
I have so much more belief,
And maybe if you believe with me, it seems
My dad will float back like a leaf.

Abby Oakley (16)
Hartshill School

Forever Perfect

I had a dream
To run like Kelly Holmes
Sing like Jennifer Lopez
For there to be no drugs, no racism, no fighting
I dream the world would be perfect
No guns, no people being killed.
To be a person that's not judged by their colour
But by who you are.

Rebecca Netherton (12)
Hartshill School

Imagine Poverty

Imagine you're someone different
Imagine you're not yourself
Imagine you live in Nigeria
Imagine you live in poverty
Imagine!
Imagine you're going to die in a week
Because this is what's happening all over the world.
Not just adults, but also children and babies.
Their lives are being lost
But we are lucky, not like them.

Rebecca Evans (12)
Hartshill School

I Am The Star

I am the star that gave you light.
I am the star that shines so bright.
I helped you gain your strength.
I am the star that gave you light.
I am the star that shines so bright.
In my dreams it is as dark as the night sky.
I shine above him with a smile and whisper goodbye.

Chelsea Lackenby (12)
Hartshill School

I Have A Dream

I dream and dream
Of pure serene
No war, no poor
Or violence and gore.

Happy children
Are soon grown men,
Life's near gone
Then stolen from.

I dream and dream
But still a dream,
Is peace and love
Of the white dove.

Emma Hall (14)
Hartshill School

My World

I hope I will never wake up
I'm here in my own world,
Thinking what I think,
No one to disturb me,
No one to stop me,
No one to tell me where to go,
No one to tell me what to do,
It's my world, just mine.

I can dream myself anywhere in the world,
I can dream what to do,
And when to do it,
But sometimes I have to wake up,
Sometimes I have to wake up,
Sometimes I have to . . .

Luke Jones (14)
Hartshill School

Dreaming Now

Dreaming now,
My thoughts and feelings,
Dreaming now,
My cures and healings,
Dreaming now,
The world is mine,
Dreaming now,
Everyone gets on,
Dreaming now,
The wars are done,
Dreaming now,
It's running away,
Dreaming done,
Another day.

Stephanie Bates (13)
Hartshill School

Dream

Imagine a world
With no famine and
Where white and black
People get along
And no racist words are heard.
There will be no war
And we will live in a quiet
And sincere community
With everyone getting along
And playing.

Callum Fawcett (13)
Hartshill School

I Had A Dream

I had a dream
The world was all peace.
I had a dream
Racism didn't exist.
I had a dream
Bullying was a crime.
I had a dream
Everyone was kind.
I had a dream
Violence was forbidden.
I had a dream
Drugs were hidden.
Have you had a dream?
That was my dream.

Laura Adey (13)
Hartshill School

I Had A Dream

I had a dream
Those racists weren't mean
I had a dream
That fights wouldn't be seen
I had a dream
That people would be keen
I had a dream
That the world would be clean
This was my dream
Is this yours?

Chloe Le-Blancq (12)
Hartshill School

Looking Out Of My Window

I look out of my window and see
I look out of my window and see sad faces,
Looking back at me.
I look out of my window and see poverty and starvation,
Drought and famine, death and destruction.

I want to look out of my window and see,
A world where people live together, without death,
Without violence and without hatred.
I want to look out of my window and see,
A country where there are no wars, no thieves and no racism.

My dream is to have a window that blanks all of these things,
My ideal window would have no racism, no thieves and no violence.
I look out of the terrible window of life.
The window that paves the way for future generations,
The window that I have grown up behind.

I want a world where it is perfect and serene,
My dream is to make the world a better place and to cut
Out all of the racist remarks and live in a world where everyone is equal.
I want to live in a world where man and woman are equal
And not treated differently.

I wish the world to be a place where everyone is the same,
Children in schools are treated no differently because of who they are.
Bullies, thieves and other offenders can be put to justice,
A place where the public can feel safe again without fret.

I look out of my window and see,
I look out of my window and see sad faces,
Looking back at me.
But I don't look out of my window and see the death and poverty,
The racism and inequality, war and suffering,
I have lived my dream looking out of my window.

Daniel Dainter (15)
Hartshill School

I Have A Dream

I have a dream
As silly as it may seem
My dream's about the world.

I dream there is joy and no pain,
Food and water, where there's no rain
I dream for freedom and the choice to speak,
Help for the poor and the weak.

I dream for safety and for care,
Across the world, make it fair.
I dream for laughter but no tears
Happy faces and lots of cheers.

I dream that there's happiness, no matter the race,
If that could happen I'd have a happy face.
I have a dream . . .
I have a dream . . .

Hannah Cooper (14)
Hartshill School

My Dreams

My dream for me
Personally
Is to be wise and clever
However
I want to inspire and invent
And for this I'm hell bent
To help mankind acquire
The ability to grow and aspire.

Now my next dream is quite chunky
As it includes the whole country
To me it seems
Our country's corrupted to the seams
By a little thing called money
It may seem funny
To hear me say this
But I do not wish
For it to stay like this
And it should change, I wish.

Now for the world, peace
Is that too much to ask?
Why can't we be friends?
Tie all those loose ends
No more fights, lies or war
Well, I mean sure
There may be the odd one
But there should be no need for bombs
We should treat each other with respect
And heck
We should help one another live
Until the end.

Ross Adams (14)
Hartshill School

I Have A Dream, Irony

I have a dream
To live on a man's settee
To rely on him for money
My friend could do better
The world won't let her
So now I'm filled with diversity.

Thousands just eat litter
Children grow no quicker
They try to call for help
The world ignores their pleas
So now we have world hunger.

People die and bombs drop faster
Hundreds injured with plaster caster
Terrorists have no shame
Countries get the blame
So now there is controversy.

If all this stopped
No killing and hunger
Doing the best you can
Not being beaten by a man
Then that would be my dream.

Jessica Bird (14)
Hartshill School

I Have A Dream

I have a dream
That everyone will be equal
That my life will have a sequel
And that this is just a prequel

I have a dream
That racism will stop
I will reach the top
And go to the university that I opt

I have a dream
That poverty will end fast
That wars won't last
And death will be a thing of the past

I have a dream
That global warming will be gone
That we will all live on
And we will be counted as one

I have a dream
That we could solve as a team
Our self-esteem we will redeem
And we won't fall apart at the seams

I have a dream . . .
I have a dream . . .

Laura Miller (13)
Hartshill School

The Day

There are people around me dreaming of the day
That fate will change and go their way
The day their dream comes true
That day when they know they'll get through
Come rain or shine
That day will be fine
When their dream comes true.

When there's nothing holding them back
And with all the confidence that they lack
They can stand up for what they believe
And say, 'I'm not going to leave
Until you all listen to what I've got to say'
This could be about white or black
With the lack
Of respect for others
Or even gay lovers
But that is what they believe in
And there is no deceiving
That some people may think they're kind of mad
But that is what they think and it's not bad.

Everyone has their day
It could be in June, April or May
But there will be a day
When your dream comes true.

Keira Shetliffe (13)
Hartshill School

I Have A Dream

I have a dream
That one day people
Will live in peace and harmony
Everyone will be happy
With no wars and no killing.

I have a dream
Where white and black people
Get on with no racial comments.

I have a dream
That there will be no poverty
No children starving or homeless.

I have a dream that we will
Never need any prisons again
All men and women
Will obey all rules.

Hayden Wright (13)
Hartshill School

I Have A Dream

I have a dream
A dream for the king and queen
I dream of a world where wealth is shared
A non-famine world
Where the word death
Will be left
I have a dream
Of no killing
And people will be willing
To listen to what is said
And that is my dream.

James McGuinness (13)
Hartshill School

I Have A Dream

I have a dream
That one day
A white person
Will be equal
To a black person
And will live in peace.

I have a dream
That nowhere
Will be poor
And the world's wealth
Will be shared.

I have a dream
That we won't
Ever need prisons again.
All men and women
Will obey laws.

Ryan Bennett (14)
Hartshill School

I Have A Dream

I have a dream
That one day everyone will be happy and peaceful
And racism will be a thing of the past
And war will never happen again
That there will be no poverty
And no children will be starving or homeless
That people will get along
And the world is calm
I have a dream.
Do you have a dream?

Calum Smith (14)
Hartshill School

Officer's Dream

I see into you all, your soul's on show to me.
I see your fear, your hatred of death,
But yet your hatred of this life.
I have a dream, each and every night in this place,
Of us, you few mortal men and I, lying on the ground
Lifeless. Our eyes forced open by the sounds of the war.
Your eyes pierce me like a pin through a balloon.
Then I'm awake.
You might think, lads, it's only a dream.
But yet, as you know and have seen
The bodies, they all lie on the mud,
Sinking slowly, absorbed by the ground,
Their eyes open as if they had been starched so.
And so, my lads, you see why I,
Your captain, cries and stutters
All night, whilst you're all gone.
My dream, you see,
Is a reality,
Since that frightful night of the Somme.

Ben Reardon (14)
King Edward VI School

I Have A Dream

I have a dream that people stop bullying and killing.
I have a dream that white people and black people love each other.
I have a dream that people stop wars.

Jonathan Newitt (13)
Oak Wood School

I Have A Dream

I have a dream
The war in Baghdad stops.
Innocent people don't get blown up
For other people's arguments.

I have a dream where
The world is free of fighting
That starvation stops
And other countries help people
Get food and water.

I have a dream
Where George Bush and Tony Blair
Pull their troops out of Iraq
And racism stops
Forever.

Tom Place (13)
Oak Wood School

Hope

I want the world to be a better place
Everyone have money, food, clothes and water.
I want Iraq to stop fighting for good
I wish people would stop taking drugs and racism to stop!

Vicky Humphrys (13)
Oak Wood School

I Have A Dream

I have a dream that there's a world with no bullying
So there's peace in the world.
I have a dream that there's no punching or kicking.
I have a dream that there's no killing people.
I have a dream that everybody helps other people.
I have a dream that nobody says 'I don't like black people'.
I have a dream that everybody's safe and sound in bed.

Stacey Harrison (14)
Oak Wood School

I Have A Dream

I have a dream
That Mummy and Daddy
Are happy together.
That Daddy calls
Me and my mum
When he gets to work.

I have a dream
For my friends
That they win at football
In Soccer's PlayStation2 game.

I have a dream
For my nana,
That she would marry Ronan Keating
And sing always.

Lina Osman (14)
Oak Wood School

I Have A Dream Where Monsters Come Alive

I have a dream where monsters come alive,
Fast cars are what they drive.
They drive within all the rules
They go and support the mighty Wolves.

I have a dream about monsters that are green,
They are kind and caring but never mean.
They help old people cross the road,
They carry their shopping so I am told.

Kieran Mancini (13)
Round Oak School & Support Service

I Have A Dream Of Being A Policeman

I have a dream of being a policeman,
I want to stop drugs and war.
I will help people when they are hurt,
And never stop being a good policeman.

I have a dream of being a policeman,
I want to stop graffiti writing and crime.
I will always make sure I'm there on time,
And never stop being a good policeman.

I have a dream of being a policeman,
I will tell people where they need to go.
I will help teenagers stop smoking,
And never stop being a good policeman.

Andrew Murray (14)
Round Oak School & Support Service

I Have A Dream Of A Better World

I have a dream to ban drugs in the world.
I have a dream to ban beer in the world.
I have a dream to ban war in the world.
I have a dream to ban killing in the world.
I have a dream to ban hunting in the world.
I have a dream to ban crime in the world.
I have a dream of a peaceful world.
I have a dream of a happy world.
I have a dream of a beautiful world.
I have a dream of a clean world.
I have a dream of a kind world
And I have a dream of a colourful world.

Terry Lee (14)
Round Oak School & Support Service

I Have A Dream

I have a dream for the world
It's a good dream.

Think of the animals
Think of all the plants
Think of the world
Think of all the pollution
Think of all the fast cars
Think of all the rubbish.

I have a dream for the world
It's a good dream.

Think of the world
Make it a better place.

Chris Cooper (14)
Round Oak School & Support Service

I Have A Dream

I have a dream and I'll tell ya what I mean.

Stop the wars!
Stop the bullying!
Stop cutting down the trees!
Future, future has begun.

Start being friendly!
Start caring for our planet!
Start looking after your family!
Future, future has begun.

Stop the fighting!
Stop the pollution!
Stop the bad language!
Future, future has begun.
Future, future has begun.

Jaspreet Reyat (12)
Round Oak School & Support Service

I Have A Dream Of Driving A Nice Car

I have a dream of driving a nice car.
I have a dream to stop people speeding.
I have a dream to go far away.
I have a dream to go to the railway.

I have a dream that people can park right.
I have a dream to go anywhere in my car.
I have a dream of having a car and it'd be white.
I have a dream of it being clean and shiny.

I have a dream and it is great!

Thomas Pugh (13)
Round Oak School & Support Service

I Have A Dream That I Will Be A Policeman

I have a dream that I will be a policeman.
I hope people will follow the rules.
I will stop people arguing and fighting
And stop cars going through red lights.

I have a dream that I will be a policeman.
I will stop drugs and drinking.
I hate racism, abuse and shootings.
I want to be an excellent policeman.

Kirt Lane (14)
Round Oak School & Support Service

I Have A Dream

Change de future!
Change de future!

No more war
No more killin'

Change de future!
Change de future!

No more robbin'
No more rudeness
No more stealin'
No more crudeness

Change de future!
Change de future!

No more bullyin'
No more being cruel
No more makin' animals de fool

Change de future!
Change de future!

Aaron Wilkinson (13)
Round Oak School & Support Service

If I Had A Dream

If I had a dream
I would like to change the whole world so there would be . . .
Less pollution,
Less litter dropping,
Less confusion.

If I had a wish
I would wish that there were no more illnesses,
No more deaths,
No more caused accidents.

If I won a lot of money
I would donate to charities.
Donate to poor countries,
Donate to save nearly the whole population.

If I could change
I would change the conflicting governments, thoughts,
I would change people's wages for more,
I would change people's thoughts to alter from bad to good.

If I could pick
I'd pick to make everything good, instead of bad.
I'd pick better hibernating homes for the wildlife.
I'd pick a life to suit everybody.

If there was a chance,
A chance to save people from being murdered.
A chance for people to have their say.
A chance to help everybody that you could.

If I had a dream
I would like to awake with all of this just not being true.

Tom Betteridge (16)
Sparrowdale School

Help

I am lying scared in a hospital bed
Thoughts going around my head.
My heart is beating
The machine is too.

I am dying and also crying,
Technology needs to move on!
Can a cure be found
For me?
For everyone?
Help!

Shivam Sanghani (16)
Sparrowdale School

My Dream

I wish the world was a better place!
No pollution
No wars
No bullies!
We are the ones who can change it!
How?
We must be strong
We must get along
Put our energy into saving the world.

Joel Titmus (15)
Sparrowdale School

My Dream

I have a dream that one day all the world will be at peace.

That there will be no more conflicts
That the world will be a better place for all of us.
I hope that the people will put down their weapons
Just think for a second!
That's my dream, I hope it comes true.

I have a dream that one day all the world will be at peace.

Callum Vickers (15)
Sparrowdale School

The Whale In The River Thames

I dream of being with my friends and family.
I dream of finding my way around and having some rest and peace.
I dream of being in a cold ocean or deep sea.
I dream of eating fish in cold water.
I dream of being rescued.
I dream of finding my way home.

Lewis Smith (14)
Sparrowdale School

The Whale's Dream

I am in the River Thames.
I dream of my family and friends.
I dream of cold ocean and deep sea.
I dream of my finding my way back home.
I dream of food and fish and water.
I dream and hope for rescue.

Nicole Griffiths (14)
Sparrowdale School

The Whale's Dream

I dream of being with my friends and family.
I dream of finding my way back home.
I dream of food and fish and cold water.
I dream of deep oceans.
I dream of finding rest and peace and quiet.
I dream of being rescued.

Emma Edwards (14)
Sparrowdale School

The Whale's Dream

I dream of my family and some friends.
I dream of cold ocean instead of this warm river.
I am hungry and thirsty.
I dream of fresh raw fish.
I am frightened and exhausted.
I am hoping to be rescued.
I dream of being safe.

Dominic James (14)
Sparrowdale School

Just Love

Wouldn't
The world
Be lovely to live in
If everybody would
Love
Each other
No more fighting
Bullying or hatred
Just
Love.

Laura Gardner (12)
Sparrowdale School

My Dream

Pollution all around
Sometimes up,
Sometimes down,
But always around.
I have a dream, pollution,
That you are no longer here
That there is a solution
To end pollution.

Michael Blower (14)
Sparrowdale School

I Wish

I wish there were no arguments, wars, fights or rows.
I wish the world were a more peaceful place to be.
I wish it were summer all the time,
Then we could go to school in a swimming pool
And our worksheets would be waterproof
And you could write on them without the ink running off.
When you are in the water you are doing English, maths
And swimming in the swimming pool at the same time
And I wish we had underwater ovens that did not conduct electricity
So you can't put your cooking in the oven while you swim underwater.

Jessica Paul (15)
Sparrowdale School

My Dream

No more family arguments.
A bit more money in my pocket.
Not being the youngest!
A home in Spain.
Keeping in touch.
Happiness.

Luke Stephens (12)
Sparrowdale School

Love

Love is a dream.
I wish I had a puppy to love.
Love is very caring.
I love my family,
All my family love me too.
I dream of love for all of you!

Kathleen Power (12)
Sparrowdale School

Zaro

Zaro came to help the people,
To make the world happy.
To make sure there were no more
Bad guys left!
He cares,
He helps,
He isn't real!
What a pity.

James Parker (13)
Sparrowdale School

Poverty

P eople will soon be dead
O f a different kind of neglect
V ery poor people
E ach trying to earn their keep
R eady to try to earn some money
T ime and time again they try to earn
Y et again, there's poverty in the world.

Scott Griffiths (14)
Sparrowdale School

Poverty

I looked at the news and what did I see?
Starving people in Africa, looking at me.
I cannot describe the look in their eyes
The trauma it gave me made me surprised.
Their pain and suffering I could briefly feel
So I turned off the TV and pretended it wasn't real.

All through the night as I tried to sleep
I could see their faces and the tears that they weep.
So I decided I had to make a stand
And take the matter into hand.
Surely someone else could see
Or is it really only me?

We just can't keep putting money into Africa's chute
We need to tackle this problem from its own grass root.
I decided to write to Tony Blair
Just to make certain he was aware.
I had to tell him there was no doubt
This problem had not been caused by a drought.

Man-made machines had destroyed their homes
And their land with little food they had grown.
Red tape and politics is what's to blame
I'm only fourteen, but I know this is insane.
Someone has got to make stand
And go and tackle this desperate land.
Or very soon, please understand
There will be no people in Africa, only derelict land!

Rebecca Swaby (15)
Trinity Catholic School